Reflections at Walden

Henry David Thoreau's Classic Writings

Reflections at Walden

Illustrated with Photographs

of Walden Pond and New England

With a Biographical Essay by Ralph Waldo Emerson

Edited by Peter Seymour

and James Morgan

♛ Hallmark Crown Editions

Francis Rogers: *Pages 4 8, 9, 19(LL,LR),*
    20(L), 26, 35, 39, 40, 52, 54, 56(LL), 61.

The Bettman Archives, Inc.: *Pages 5, 6.*

Reverend Herman Bielenberg: *Page 21.*

Martin Bordner: *Page 27(L).*

Ron Brown: *Title Page (R).*

Dr. E. R. Degginger: *Pages 27(R), 31(LL), 37,*
    38(L), 51(R), 56(UL,UR,LR).

Richard Fanolio: *Pages 19(UR), 22, 45.*

Carter L. Hamilton: *Pages 25, 38(R), 42, 60(L).*

Dan Havner: *Page 51(L).*

Joe Klemovich: *Page 28.*

John Kohout, Root Resources: *Page 31(LR).*

James Lipp: *Pages 15, 29, 32, 48, 60(R).*

Peveril Meigs: *Page 50.*

Sue Morey: *Page 31(UL,UR).*

Charles R. Potter, FPG: *Endpapers.*

Roland Wells Robbins: *Page 13.*

Robert S. Ross: *Page 19(UL).*

Phil Smith: *Pages 16, 47, 58.*

Joe Van Dolah: *Title Page (L), Dust Jacket, Page 10.*

Dr. John Weaver: *Page 46.*

Lyle Wessale: *Page 20(R).*

Set in Linotype Aldus, by Rochester Typographic Service.
Photographic Supervision by Francis Rogers.
Designed by William M. Gilmore.

CONTENTS

HENRY DAVID THOREAU
by Ralph Waldo Emerson

Henry David Thoreau (1817-1862)

Thoreau is buried in Concord's Sleepy Hollow cemetery, near the woods in which he lived.

Henry David Thoreau was the last male descendant of a French ancestor who came to this country from the Isle of Guernsey. His character exhibited occasional traits drawn from this blood in singular combination with a very strong Saxon genius.

He was born in Concord, Massachusetts, on the 12th of July, 1817. He was graduated at Harvard College in 1837, but without any literary distinction. After leaving the University, he joined his brother in teaching a private school, which he soon renounced. His father was a manufacturer of lead-pencils, and Henry applied himself for a time to this craft, believing he could make a better pencil than was then in use. After completing his experiments, he exhibited his work to chemists and artists in Boston, and having obtained their certificates to its excellence and to its equality with the best London manufacture, he returned home contented. His friends congratulated him that he had now opened his way to fortune. But he replied that he should never make another pencil. "Why should I? I would not do again what I have done once." He resumed his endless walks and miscellaneous studies, making every day some new acquaintance with nature, though as yet never speaking of zoology or botany, since, though very studious of natural facts, he was incurious of technical and textual science. He declined to give up his large ambition of knowledge and action for any narrow craft or profession, aiming at a much more comprehensive calling, the art of living well.

He was bred to no profession; he never married; he lived alone; he never went to church; he never voted; he refused to pay a tax to the State; he ate no flesh, he drank no wine, he never knew the use of tobacco; and, though a naturalist, he used neither trap nor gun. He chose, wisely, no doubt, for himself, to be the bachelor of thought and nature.

Hermit and stoic as he was, he threw himself heartily and child-like into the company of young people whom he loved, and whom he delighted to entertain, as he only could, with the varied and end-less anecdotes of his experiences by field and river.

No truer American existed than Thoreau. His preference of his country and condition was genuine, and his aversation from English and European manners and tastes almost reached contempt. . . . But idealist as he was, standing for abolition of slavery, abolition of tariffs, almost for abolition of government, it is needless to say he found himself not only unrepresented in actual politics, but almost equally opposed to every class of reformers. Mr. Thoreau was equipped with a most adapted and serviceable body. He was of short stature, firmly built, of light complexion, with strong, serious blue eyes, and a grave aspect—his face covered in the late years with a becoming beard. His senses were acute, his frame well-knit and hardy, his hands strong and skillful in the use of tools.

Mr. Thoreau dedicated his genius with such entire love to the fields, hills, and waters of his native town, that he made them known and interesting to all reading Americans, and to people over the sea. . . . It was a pleasure and a privilege to walk with him. He knew the country like a fox or a bird, and passed through it as freely by paths of his own. He knew every track in the snow or on the ground, and what creatures had taken this path before him. One must submit abjectly to such a guide, and the reward was great. Under his arm he carried an old music-book to press plants; in his pocket, his diary and pencil, a spy-glass for birds, microscope, jack-knife and twine.

He loved nature so well, was so happy in her solitude, that he became very jealous of cities, and the sad work which their refinements and artifices made with man and his dwelling. . . . His soul was made for the noblest society; he had in a short life exhausted the capabilities of this world. Wherever there is knowledge, wherever there is virtue, wherever there is beauty, he will find a home.

This sketch of Thoreau at age 37 was drawn by one of his contemporaries, D. Ricketson.

REFLECTIONS AT WALDEN

From WALDEN, OR LIFE IN THE WOODS

In the spring of 1845 Thoreau began building a cabin by Walden Pond, about two miles from Concord, on property owned by Emerson. Thoreau moved in on July 4. His intention was "to drive life into a corner, and to reduce it to its lowest terms." Here he describes how he lived and what he gained from his two years in the woods. The selections that follow have been condensed and rearranged.

When I wrote the following pages, or rather the bulk of them, I lived alone, in the woods, a mile from any neighbor, in a house which I had built myself, on the shore of Walden Pond, in Concord, Massachusetts, and earned my living by the labor of my hands only. I lived there two years and two months.

Near the end of March, 1845, I borrowed an axe and went down to the woods by Walden Pond, nearest to where I intended to build my house, and began to cut down some tall, arrowy white pines, still in their youth, for timber. . . . It was a pleasant hillside where I worked, covered with pine woods, through which I looked out on the pond, and a small open field in the woods where pines and hickories were springing up. The ice in the pond was not yet dissolved, though there were open spaces, and it was all dark-colored and saturated with water. They were pleasant spring days, in which the winter of man's discontent was thawing as well as the earth, and the life that had lain torpid began to stretch itself out.

The original location of Thoreau's house was discovered in 1945 by Roland Wells Robbins. Today the site is marked by rocks from the house's foundation.

At length, in the beginning of May, with the help of some of my acquaintances, rather to improve so good an occasion for neighborliness than from necessity, I set up the frame of my house.

Before winter I built a chimney, and shingled the sides of my house, which were already impervious to rain. I have thus a tight shingled and plastered house, ten feet wide by fifteen long, with a garret and a closet, a large window on each side, two trap-doors, one door at each end, and a brick fireplace opposite. The exact cost of my house, paying the usual price for such materials as I used, but not counting the work, all of which was done by myself, was: $28.12½.

I give the details because very few are able to tell exactly what their houses cost, and fewer still, if any, the separate cost of the various materials which compose them:—

Boards	$ 8.03 ½, mostly shanty boards.
Refuse shingles for roof and sides	4.00
Laths	1.25
Two second-hand windows with glass	2.43 4.00
One thousand old brick	2.40 That was high.
Two casks of lime	0.31 More than I needed.
Hair	0.15
Mantle-tree iron	3.90
Nails	0.14
Hinges and screws	0.10
Latch	0.01
Chalk	1.40 I carried a good part
Transportation	on my back.
In all	$28.12 ½

I did not read books the first summer; I hoed beans. Nay, I often did better than this. There were times when I could not afford to sacrifice the bloom of the present moment to any work, whether of head or hands. I love a broad margin to my life. Sometimes, in a summer morning, having taken my accustomed bath, I sat in my sunny doorstep from sunrise till noon, rapt in a revery, amidst the pines and hickories and sumachs, in undisturbed solitude and still-ness, while the birds sang around or flitted noiseless through the

This reconstruction of Thoreau's house was built from Thoreau's own description in Walden. *It stands in Lincoln, Massachusetts, near the home of Roland Wells Robbins.*

house, until by the sun falling in at my west window, or the noise of some traveller's wagon on the distant highway, I was reminded of the lapse of time. I grew in those seasons like corn in the night, and they were far better than any work of the hands would have been.

I had this advantage, at least, in my mode of life, over those who were obliged to look abroad for amusement, to society and the theater, that my life itself was become my amusement and never ceased to be novel. It was a drama of many scenes and without an end.

'I LOVE THE WILD'

My furniture, part of which I made myself, consisted of a bed, a table, a desk, three chairs, a looking glass three inches in diameter, a pair of tongs and andirons, a kettle, a skillet, and a frying pan, a dipper, a washbowl, two knives and forks, three plates, one cup, one spoon, a jug for oil, a jug for molasses, and a japanned lamp. None is so poor that he need sit on a pumpkin. This is shiftlessness.

When first I took up my abode in the woods, that is, began to spend my nights as well as my days there, which, by accident, was on Independence Day, or the Fourth of July, 1845, my house was not finished for winter, but was merely a defence against the rain, without plastering or chimney, the walls being of rough, weather-stained boards, with wide chinks, which made it cool at night. I did not need to go outdoors to take the air, for the atmosphere within had lost none of its freshness.

I went to the woods because I wished to live deliberately, to front only the essential facts of life, and see if I could not learn what it had to teach, and not, when I came to die, discover that I had not lived. I did not wish to live what was not life, living is so dear; nor did I wish to practice resignation, unless it was quite necessary. I wanted to live deep and suck out all the marrow of life, to live so sturdily and Spartan-like as to put to rout all that was not life, to cut a broad swath and shave close, to drive life into a corner, and reduce it to its lowest terms, and, if it proved to be mean, why then to get the whole and genuine meanness of it, and publish its meanness to the world; or if it were sublime, to know it by experience, and be able to give a true account of it in my next excursion.

Every morning was a cheerful invitation to make my life of equal simplicity, and I may say innocence, with nature herself.

Once or twice, I found myself ranging the woods, like a half-starved hound, with a strange abandonment, seeking some kind of venison which I might devour, and no morsel could have been too savage for me. The wildest scenes had become unaccountably familiar. I found in myself, and still find, an instinct toward a higher, or, as it is named, spiritual life, as do most men, and another toward a primitive rank and savage one, and I reverence them both. I love the wild not less than the good. The wildness and adventure that are in fishing still recommend it to me. I like sometimes to take rank hold on life and spend my day more as animals do.

Regularly at half-past seven, in one part of the summer, the whip-poor-wills chanted their vespers for half an hour, sitting on a stump by my door, or upon the ridge-pole of the house. When other birds are still, the screech owls take up the strain, like mourning women their ancient u-lu-lu. Wise midnight hags!

'WALDEN WEARS BEST'

This is a delicious evening, when the whole body is one sense, and imbibes delight through every pore. I go and come with a strange liberty in nature, a part of herself. There can be no very black melancholy to him who lives in the midst of nature and has his senses still.

Some of my pleasantest hours were during the long rainstorms in the spring or fall, which confined me to the house for the afternoon

as well as the forenoon, soothed by their ceaseless roar and pelting; when an early twilight ushered in a long evening in which many thoughts had time to take root and unfold themselves. In those driving northeast rains which tried the village houses so, when the maids stood ready with mop and pail in front entries to keep the deluge out, I sat behind my door in my little house, which was all entry, and thoroughly enjoyed its protection. In one heavy thunder-shower the lightning struck a large pitch pine across the pond, making a very conspicuous and perfectly regular spiral groove from top to bottom, an inch or more deep, and four or five inches wide, as you would groove a walking-stick.

Men frequently say to me, "I should think you would feel lonesome down there, and want to be nearer to folks, rainy and snowy days and nights especially." I am tempted to reply to such,—This whole earth which we inhabit is but a point in space. How far apart, think you, dwell the two most distant inhabitants of yonder star? Why should I feel lonely? Is not our planet in the Milky Way?

I had three chairs in my house; one for solitude, two for friendship, three for society. One inconvenience I sometimes experienced in so small a house, the difficulty of getting to a sufficient distance from my guest when we began to utter big thoughts in big words. You want room for your thoughts to get into sailing trim and run a course or two before they make their port.

In warm evening I frequently sat in my boat playing the flute, and saw the perch, which I seem to have charmed, hovering around me, and the moon travelling over the ribbed bottom, which was strewn with the wrecks of the forest. Formerly, I had come to this pond adventurously, from time to time, in dark summer nights, with a companion, and, making a fire close to the water's edge, which we thought attracted the fishes, we caught pouts with a bunch of worms strung on a thread, and when we had done, far into the night, threw the burning brands high into the air like skyrockets, which, coming down into the pond, were quenched with a loud hissing, and we were suddenly in total darkness.

...the first light dawned on the earth, and the birds awoke....

Of all the characters I have known, perhaps Walden wears best, the best preserves its purity. Many men have been likened to it, but few deserve the honor. Though the woodchoppers have laid bare first this shore and then that, and the Irish have built their sties by it, and the railroad has infringed on its border, and the icemen have skimmed it once, it is itself unchanged; all the change is in me. It has not acquired one permanent wrinkle after all its ripples. It is perennially young.

CONCLUSION

I left the woods for as good a reason as I went there. Perhaps it seemed to me that I had several more lives to live, and could not spare any more time for that one. It is remarkable how easily and sensibly we fall into a particular route, and make a beaten track for ourselves. I had not lived there a week before my feet wore a path from my door to the pondside; and though it is five or six years since I trod it, it is still quite distinct. I learned this at least, by my experiment; that if one advances confidently in the direction of his dreams, and endeavors to live the life which he has imagined, he will meet with a success unexpected in common hours. In proportion as he simplifies his life, the laws of the universe will appear less complex, and solitude will not be solitude, nor poverty poverty, nor weakness weakness. If you have built castles in the air, your work need not be lost; that is where they should be. Now put the foundations under them.

Why should we be in such desperate haste to succeed and in such desperate enterprises? If a man does not keep pace with his companions, perhaps it is because he hears a different drummer. Let him step to the music which he hears, however measured or far away.

Every morning was a cheerful invitation to make my life
of equal simplicity, and I may say innocence, with Nature herself.

It is not important that he should mature as soon as an apple tree or an oak. Shall he turn his spring into summer? If the conditions of things which we were made for is not yet, what were any reality which we can substitute? We will not be shipwrecked on a vain reality.

I do not say that John or Jonathan will realize all this; but such is the character of that morrow which mere lapse of time can never make to dawn. The light which puts out our eyes is darkness to us. Only that day dawns to which we are awake. There is more day to dawn. The sun is but a morning star.

From A WEEK ON THE CONCORD
AND MERRIMACK RIVERS

Of the river, Thoreau wrote: "At last I resolved to launch myself on its bosom and float whither it would bear me." Over a ten-year period he worked to expand the journal of the trip, making final editorial revisions at Walden Pond. The book was published in 1849; appreciative reviews followed, but few sales.

Sometimes,

in a summer morning, I sat

in my sunny doorstep from

sunrise till noon, rapt

in a revery, amidst the pines

and hickories and sumachs,

in undisturbed solitude and

stillness, while the birds sang....

SATURDAY: At length, on Saturday, the last day of August, 1839, we two, brothers and natives of Concord, weighed anchor in this river port. Our boat was in form like a fisherman's dory, fifteen feet long by three and a half in breadth at the widest part, painted green below, with a border of blue, with reference to the two elements in which it was to spend its existence. A warm, drizzling rain had obscured the morning, but at length the leaves and grass were dried, and it came out a mild afternoon. So with a vigorous shove we launched our boat from the bank, while the flags and bulrushes curtsied a God-speed, and dropped silently down the stream. Gradually the village murmur subsided, and we seemed to be embarked on the placid current of our dreams, floating from past to future as silently as one awakes to fresh morning or evening thoughts. We contemplated at our leisure the lapse of the river and of human life; and as that current, with its floating twigs and leaves, so did all things pass in review before us. There is, indeed, a tide in the affairs of men, as the poet says, and yet as things flow they circulate, and the ebb always balances the flow. All streams are but tributary to the ocean, which itself does not stream, and the shores are unchanged, but in longer periods than man can measure. Go where we will, we discover infinite changes in particulars only, not in generals.

SUNDAY: In the morning the river and adjacent country were covered with a dense fog, through which the smoke of our fire curled up like a still subtiler mist; but before we had rowed many rods, the sun arose and the fog rapidly dispersed, leaving a slight steam only to curl along the surface of the water.

By noon we were let down into the Merrimack through the locks at Middlesex, just above Pawtucket Falls, by a serene and liberal-minded man, who came quietly from his book, though his duties, we supposed, did not require him to open the locks on Sundays. With him we had a just and equal encounter of the eyes, as between two honest men.

MONDAY: When the first light dawned on the earth, and the birds awoke, and the brave river was heard rippling confidently seaward, and the nimble early rising wind rustled the oak leaves about our tent, all men, having reinforced their bodies and their souls with sleep, and cast aside doubt and fear, were invited to unattempted adventures.

The wilderness is near as well as dear to every man. Even the oldest villages are indebted to the border of wild wood which surrounds them, more than to the gardens of men. There is something indescribably inspiriting and beautiful in the aspect of the forest skirting and occasionally jutting into the midst of new towns, which, like the sand-heaps of fresh fox-burrows, have sprung up in their midst. The very uprightness of the pines and maples asserts the ancient rectitude and vigor of nature. Our lives need the relief of such a background, where the pine flourishes and the jay still screams.

TUESDAY: We rowed for some hours between glistening banks trickling with water. Sometimes this purer and cooler water, bursting out from under a pine or a rock, was collected into a basin close to the edge of and level with the river. So near along life's stream are the fountains of innocence and youth making fertile its sandy margin; and the voyager will do well to replenish his vessels often at these uncontaminated sources.

There were several canal-boats at Cromwell's Falls passing through the locks, for which we waited.

In the forward part of one stood a brawny New Hampshire man,

It seems to take but one summer day to fetch the summer in.

leaning on his pole. He inquired, just as we were passing out of earshot, if we had killed anything, and we shouted after him that we had shot a buoy, and could see him for a long while scratching his head in vain to know if he had heard aright.

WEDNESDAY: While we float here, far from that tributary stream on whose banks our friends and kindred dwell, our thoughts, like the stars, come out of their horizon still. After years of vain familiarity, some distant gesture or unconscious behavior, which we remember, speaks to us with more emphasis than the wisest or kindest words. We are sometimes made aware of a kindness long passed, and realize that there have been times when our friends' thoughts of us were of so pure and lofty a character that they passed over us like the winds of heaven unnoticed; when they treated us not as what we were, but as what we aspired to be. Friendship is evanescent in every man's experience, and remembered like heat lightning in past summers. Fair and flitting like a summer cloud—there is always some vapor in the air, no matter how long the drought.

Summer is gone with all its
infinite wealth, and still nature
is genial to man. Though he
no longer bathes in the stream,
or reclines on the bank, or plucks
berries on the hills, still he
beholds the same inaccessible
beauty around him.

28

THURSDAY: The rain had pattered all night, and now the whole country wept. We managed to keep our thoughts dry, however, and only our clothes were wet. We no longer sailed or floated on the river, but trod the unyielding land like pilgrims. And we found that the frontiers had changed. Go where we will on the *surface* of things, men have been there before us. The frontiers are not east or west, north or south; but wherever a man *fronts* a fact.

FRIDAY: As the truest society approaches always nearer to solitude, so the most excellent speech finally falls into silence. Silence is audible to all men, at all times, and in all places. She is when we hear inwardly, sound when we hear outwardly. Creation has not displaced her, but is her visible framework and foil. All sounds are her servants, and purveyors, proclaiming not only that their mistress is, but is a rare mistress, and earnestly to be sought after. Silence is the universal refuge, the sequel to all dull discourses and all foolish acts, a balm to our every chagrin, as welcome after satiety as after disappointment. It were vain for me to endeavor to interpret the Silence. She cannot be done into English.

We had made about fifty miles this day with sail and oar, and now, far in the evening, our boat was grating against the bulrushes of its native port, and its keel recognized the Concord mud, where some semblance of its outline was still preserved in the flattened flags which had scarce yet erected themselves since our departure; and we leaped gladly on shore, drawing it up and fastening it to the wild apple tree, whose stem still bore the mark which its chain had worn in the chafing of the spring freshets.

Color stands for all ripeness and success....The very forest and herbage,
the pellicle of the earth as it were, must acquire a bright color, an evidence of its ripeness,
as if the globe itself were a fruit on its stem, with ever one cheek toward the sun.

POEMS

Thoreau's early poetry first attracted Ralph Waldo Emerson's attention to the young man. Later, Emerson would decide that the verse did not live up to expectation, and Thoreau would rashly destroy all but his earliest works. The several early poems that survive are interesting records of a young man's initiation into nature.

THE RESPECTABLE FOLKS

The respectable folks—
Where dwell they?
They whisper in the oaks,
And they sigh in the hay;
Summer and winter, night and day,
Out on the meadow, there dwell they.
They never die,
Nor snivel, nor cry,
Nor ask our pity
With a wet eye.
A sound estate they ever mind,
To every asker readily lend;
To the ocean wealth,
To the meadow health,
To Time his length,
To the rocks strength,
To the stars light,
To the weary night,
To the busy day,
To the idle play;
And so their good cheer never ends,
For all are their debtors, and all their friends.

The very uprightness of the pines and maples asserts the ancient rectitude and vigor of Nature. Our lives need the relief of such a background, where the pine flourishes and the jay still screams.

SIC VITA

I am a parcel of vain strivings tied
    By a chance bond together,
Dangling this way and that, their links
    Were made so loose and wide,
      Methinks,
    For milder weather.

A bunch of violets without their roots,
    And sorrel intermixed,
Encircled by a wisp of straw
    Once coiled about their shoots,
      The law
    By which I'm fixed.

A nosegay which Time clutched from out
    Those fair Elysian fields,
With weeds and broken stems, in haste,
    Doth make the rabble rout
      That waste
    The day he yields.

And here I bloom for a short hour unseen,
    Drinking my juices up,
With no root in the land
    To keep my branches green,
      But stand
    In a bare cup.

Some tender buds were left upon my stem
    In mimicry of life,
But ah! the children will not know
    Till time has withered them,
      The woe
    With which they're rife.

But now I see I was not plucked for naught,
    And after in life's vase
Of glass set while I might survive,
    But by a kind hand brought
      Alive
    To a strange place.

That stock thus thinned will soon redeem its hours,
    And by another year,
Such as God knows, with freer air,
    More fruits and fair flowers
      Will bear,
    While I droop here.

MY PRAYER

Great God, I ask thee for no meaner pelf
Than that I may not disappoint myself;
That in my action I may soar as high
As I can now discern with this clear eye.

And next in value, which they kindness lends,
That I may greatly disappoint my friends,
Howe'er they think or hope that it may be,
They may not dream how thou'st distinguished me.

That my weak hand may equal my firm faith,
And my life practice more than my tongue saith;
    That my low conduct may not show,
      Nor my relenting lines,
    That I thy purpose did not know,
      Or overrated thy designs.

It is so long since I have heard it
that the steady, soaking, rushing
sound of the rain on the shingles
is musical. . . . The sound soaks into
my spirit, as the water into the earth,
reminding me of the season when
snow and ice will be no more,
when the earth will be thawed and
drink up the rain as fast as it falls.

MEN SAY
THEY KNOW MANY THINGS

Men say they know many things;
But lo! they have taken wings—
The arts and sciences,
And a thousand appliances;
The wind that blows
Is all that any body knows.

There were times when I could not afford to sacrifice the bloom
of the present moment to any work.

From THE JOURNAL

Throughout his adult life Thoreau kept an almost daily account of everything he saw, did and thought about. This was his Journal, *most of which has been published in fourteen volumes. The Journal covers the vast ranges of Thoreau's thoughts, offering a multitude of observations on life and colorful portraits of nature.*

OBSERVATIONS ON LIFE

I think that we are not commonly aware that man is our contemporary—that in this strange, outlandish world, so barren, so prosaic, fit not to live in but merely to pass through, that even here so divine a creature as man does actually live. Man, the crowning fact, the god we know. While the earth supports so rare an inhabitant, there is somewhat to cheer us. Who shall say that there is no God, if there is a *just* man?

The intellect of most men is barren. They neither fertilize nor are fertilized. It is the marriage of the soul with nature that makes the intellect fruitful, that gives birth to imagination.

It seems to take but one summer day to fetch the summer in.

Like cuttlefish we conceal ourselves, we darken the atmosphere in which we move; we are not transparent. I pine for one to whom I can speak my *first thoughts;* thoughts which represent me truly, which are no better and no worse than I; thoughts which have the bloom on them, which alone can be sacred or divine.

There is, indeed, a tide in the affairs of men, as the poet says, and yet as things flow they circulate, and the ebb always balances the flow. . . . Go where we will, we discover infinite changes in particulars only, not in generals.

October answers to that period in the life of man when he is no longer dependent on his transient moods, when all his experience ripens into wisdom. . . .

Cultivate reverence. It is as if you were so much more respectable yourself. By the quality of a man's writing, by the elevation of its tone, you may measure his self-respect. How shall a man continue his culture after manhood?

Do not tread on the heels of your experience. Be impressed without making a minute of it. Poetry puts an interval between the impression and the expression—waits till the seed germinates naturally.

We believe that the possibility of the future far exceeds the accomplishment of the past. We review the past with the common sense, but we anticipate the future with transcendental senses. In our sanest moments we find ourselves naturally expecting or prepared for far greater changes than any which we have experienced within the period of distinct memory, only to be paralleled by experiences which are forgotten. Perchance there are revolutions which create an interval impassable to the memory.

Perhaps what most moves us in winter is some reminiscence of far-off summer. For we are hunters pursuing the summer on snow-shoes and skates, all winter long. There is really but one season in our hearts.

My townsmen have been shooting and trapping musquash and mink. Am not I a trapper too, setting my traps in solitude, and baiting them as well as I know how, that I may catch life and light, that my intellectual part may taste some venison and be invigorated, that my nakedness may be clad in some wild, furry warmth?

Love is a mutual confidence whose foundations no one knows. The one I love surpasses all the laws of nature in sureness. Love is capable of any wisdom.

However mean your life is, meet it and live; do not shun it and call it hard names. It is not so bad as you are. It looks poorest when you are richest. The fault-finder will find faults even in paradise. Love your life, poor as it is.

If a man has spent all his days about some business, by which he has merely got to be rich, as it is called, *i.e.*, has got much money, many houses and barns and woodlots, then his life has been a failure, I think; but if he has been trying to better his condition in a higher sense than this, has been trying to invent something, to be somebody—*i.e.*, to invent and get a patent for himself—so that all may see his originality, though he should never get above board—and great inventors, you know, commonly die poor—I shall think him comparatively successful.

PORTRAITS OF NATURE

Summer is gone with all its infinite wealth, and still nature is genial to man. Though he no longer bathes in the stream, or reclines on the bank, or plucks berries on the hills, still he beholds the same inaccessible beauty around him.

October answers to that period in the life of man when he is no longer dependent on his transient moods, when all his experience ripens into wisdom, but every root, branch, leaf of him glows with maturity. What he has been and done in his spring and summer appears. He bears his fruit.

If I were to paint the short days of winter, I should represent two towering icebergs, approaching each other like promontories, for morning and evening, with cavernous recesses, and a solitary traveller, wrapping his cloak about him and bent forward against a driving storm, just entering the narrow pass. I would paint the light of a taper at midday, seen through a cottage window half buried in snow and frost, and some pale stars in the sky, and the sound of the woodcutter's axe. The icebergs with cavernous recesses. In the foreground, through the pass, should be seen the sowers in the fields and other evidences of spring. The icebergs should gradually approach, and on the right and left the heavens should be shaded off from the light of midday to midnight with its stars. The sun low in the sky.

Silence is audible to all men,
at all times, and in all places.
She is when we hear inwardly,
sound when we hear outwardly.

This is a delicious evening, when the whole body is one sense,
and imbibes delight through every pore. I go and come
with a strange liberty in Nature, a part of herself.
There can be no very black melancholy to him who lives
in the midst of Nature....

I was...serenaded by a hooting owl. I rejoice that
there are owls....They represent the stark twilight and
unsatisfied thoughts which all have.

It is so long since I have heard it that the steady, soaking, rushing sound of the rain on the shingles is musical. The fire needs no replenishing, and we save our fuel. It seems like a distant forerunner of spring. It is because I am allied to the elements that the sound of the rain is thus soothing to me. The sound soaks into my spirit, as the water into the earth, reminding me of the season when snow and ice will be no more, when the earth will be thawed and drink up the rain as fast as it falls.

Is not the dew but a humbler, gentler rain, the nightly rain, above which we raise our heads and unobstructedly behold the stars? The mountains are giants which tower above the rain, as we above the dew in the grass; it only wets their feet.

I pass the pond in the road, I see the sun, which is about entering the grosser hazy atmosphere above the western horizon, brilliantly reflected in the pond—a dazzling sheen, a bright golden shimmer. His broad sphere extended stretches the whole length of the pond toward me.

Saw to-day for the first time this season fleets of yellow butterflies dispersing before us. . . . Like a mackerel fleet, with their small hulls and great sails. Collected now in compact but gorgeous assembly in the road, like schooners in a harbor, a haven; now suddenly dispersing on our approach and filling the air with yellow snowflakes in their zigzag flight, or as when a fair wind calls those schooners out and disperses them over the broad ocean.

The roar of the wind over the pines sounds like the surf on countless beaches, an endless shore; and at intervals it sounds like a gong resounding through halls and entries, *i.e.,* there is a certain resounding woodiness in the tone. How the wind roars among the shrouds of the wood!

Nature now, like an athlete, begins to strip herself in earnest for her contest with her great antagonist Winter. In the bare trees and twigs what a display of muscle!

*Men frequently say to me,
"I should think you would feel
lonesome down there, and want
to be nearer to folks, rainy and
snowy days and nights especially."
I am tempted to reply to such—
this whole earth which
we inhabit is but a point in space.
How far apart, think you, dwell
the two most distant inhabitants
of yonder star? Why should I
feel lonely? Is not our planet
in the Milky Way?*

Why do you flee so soon, sir, to the theaters, lecture-rooms, and museums
of the city? If you will stay here awhile I will promise you strange sights.
You shall walk on water; all these brooks and rivers and ponds shall be your highway.
You shall see the whole earth covered a foot or more deep
with purest white crystals, in which you slump or over which you glide,
and all the trees and stubble glittering in icy armor.

Nature...is ever in her spring, where the moss-grown and
decaying trees are not old, but seem to enjoy a perpetual youth; and blissful,
innocent Nature, like a serene infant, is too happy to make a noise,
except by a few tinkling, lisping birds and trickling rills....

I saw in the northwest first rise, in the rose-tinted horizon sky, a dark, narrow, craggy cloud, narrow and projecting as no cloud on earth, seen against the rose-tinted sky—the crest of a thunderstorm, beautiful and grand.

The brilliant autumnal colors are red and yellow and the various tints, hues, and shades of these. Blue is reserved to be the color of the sky, but yellow and red are the colors of the earth flower. Every fruit, on ripening, and just before its fall, acquires a bright tint. So do the leaves; so the sky before the end of the day, and the year near its setting. October is the red sunset sky, November the later twilight. Color stands for all ripeness and success. . . . The very forest and herbage, the pellicle of the earth as it were, must acquire a bright color, an evidence of its ripeness, as if the globe itself were a fruit on its stem, with ever one cheek toward the sun.

Why do you flee so soon, sir, to the theaters, lecture-rooms, and museums of the city? If you will stay here awhile I will promise you strange sights. You shall walk on water; all these brooks and rivers and ponds shall be your highway. You shall see the whole earth covered a foot or more deep with purest white crystals, in which you slump or over which you glide, and all the trees and stubble glittering in icy armor.

I saw the reflections of the moon sliding down the watery concave like so many lustrous burnished coins poured from a bag with inexhaustible lavishness, and the lambent flames on the surface were much multiplied, seeming to slide along a few inches with each wave before they were extinguished.

53

The bluebird which some woodchopper or inspired walker is said to have seen in that sunny interval between the snowstorms is like a speck of clear blue sky seen near the end of a storm, reminding us of an ethereal region and a heaven which we had forgotten. Princes and magistrates are often styled serene, but what is their turbid serenity to that ethereal serenity which the bluebird embodies? His Most Serene Birdship! His soft warble melts in the ear, as the snow is melting in the valleys around.

What a world we live in! Where myriads of these little disks, so beautiful to the most prying eye, are whirled down on every traveler's coat, the observant and the unobservant, and on the restless squirrel's fur, and on the far-stretching fields and forests, the wooded dells, and the mountain-tops. Far, far away from the haunts of man, they roll down some little slope, fall over and come to their bearings, and melt or lose their identity in the mass, ready anon to swell some little rill with their contribution, and so, at last, the universal ocean from which they came. There they lie, like the wreck of chariot-wheels after a battle in the skies. Meanwhile the meadow mouse shoves them aside in his gallery, the schoolboy casts them in his snowball, or the woodsman's sled glides smoothly over them, these glorious spangles, the sweeping of heaven's floor. And they all sing, melting as they sing of the mysteries of the number six—six, six, six. He takes up the water of the sea in his hand, leaving the salt; He disperses it in mist through the skies; He recollects and sprinkles it like grain in six-rayed snowy stars over the earth, there to lie till He dissolves its bonds again.

Perhaps what most moves us in winter is some reminiscence of far-off summer. For we are hunters pursuing the summer on snow-shoes and skates, all winter long. There is really but one season in our hearts.

From KTAADN AND
THE MAINE WOODS

Thoreau published this article in 1858 in The Union Magazine. *Horace Greeley helped Thoreau sell it—for $75.00. The narrative describes Thoreau's first visit, in September of 1846, into the rugged Maine woods and his ascent of Mt. Ktaadn, the second highest mountain in the New England states.*

I climbed alone over huge rocks, loosely poised, a mile or more, still edging toward the clouds; for. though the day was clear elsewhere, the summit was concealed by mist. The mountain seemed a vast aggregation of loose rocks, as if some time it had rained rocks, and they lay as they fell on the mountain sides, nowhere fairly at rest, but leaning on each other, all rocking stones, with cavities between, but scarcely any soil or smoother shelf. They were the raw materials of a planet dropped from an unseen quarry, which the vast chemistry of nature would anon work up, or work down, into the smiling and verdant plains and valleys of earth. This was an undone extremity of the globe; as in lignite we see coal in the process of formation.

I had this advantage . . . in my mode of life, over those who were obliged to look abroad for amusement, to society and the theater, that my life itself was become my amusement and never ceased to be novel.
It was a drama of many scenes and without an end.

She does not smile on him as in the plains. She seems to say sternly, Why came ye here before your time. This ground is not prepared for you. Is it not enough that I smile in the valleys? I have never made this soil for thy feet, this air for thy breathing, these rocks for thy neighbors. I cannot pity nor fondle thee here, but forever relentlessly drive thee hence to where I *am* kind. Why seek me where I have not called thee, and then complain because you find me but a stepmother? Shouldst thou freeze or starve, or shudder thy life away, here is no shrine, nor altar, nor any access to my ear.

It reminded me of the creations of the old epic and dramatic poets, of Atlas, Vulcan, the Cyclops, and Prometheus. Such was Caucasus

Of all the characters I have known, perhaps Walden
wears best, the best preserves its purity. Many men have
been likened to it, but few deserve the honor.
Though the woodchoppers have laid bare first this shore
and then that, and the Irish have built their sties by it,
and the railroad has infringed on its border,
and the icemen have skimmed it once, it is itself
unchanged; all the change is in me. It has not acquired
one permanent wrinkle after all its ripples.
It is perennially young.

and the rock where Prometheus was bound. Aeschylus had no doubt visited such scenery as this. It was vast, Titanic, and such as man never inhabits. Some part of the beholder, even some vital part, seems to escape through the loose grating of his ribs as he ascends. He is more lone than you can imagine. There is less of substantial thought and fair understanding in him than in the plains where men inhabit. His reason is dispersed and shadowy, more thin and subtle, like the air. Vast, Titanic, inhuman Nature has got him at disadvantage, caught him alone, and pilfers him of some of his divine faculty.

At length I entered within the skirts of the cloud which seemed forever drifting over the summit, and yet would never be gone, but was generated out of that pure air as fast as it flowed away; and when, a quarter of a mile farther, I reached the summit of the ridge, which those who have seen it in clearer weather say is about five miles long, and contains a thousand acres of table-land, I was deep within the hostile ranks of clouds, and all objects were obscured by them. Now the wind would blow me out a yard of clear sunlight, wherein I stood; then a gray, dawning light was all it could accomplish, the

cloud-line ever rising and falling with the wind's intensity. Sometimes it seemed as if the summit would be cleared in a few moments,
and smile in sunshine; but what was gained on one side was lost
on another.

Maine is a country full of evergreen trees, of mossy silver birches
and watery maples, the ground dotted with insipid small, red berries, and strewn with damp and moss-grown rocks—a country di-
versified with innumerable lakes and rapid streams, peopled with
trout and various species of *leucisci*, with salmon, shad, and pick-
erel, and other fishes; the forest resounding at rare intervals with
the note of the chickadee, the blue jay, and the woodpecker, the
scream of the fish hawk and the eagle, the laugh of the loon, and
the whistle of ducks along the solitary streams; at night, with the
hooting of owls and howling of wolves; in summer, swarming with
myriads of black flies and mosquitoes, more formidable than wolves
to the white man.

Such is the home of the moose, the bear, the caribou, the wolf, the beaver, and the Indian. Who shall describe the inexpressible tenderness and immortal life of the grim forest, where Nature, though it be midwinter, is ever in her spring, where the moss-grown and decaying trees are not old, but seem to enjoy a perpetual youth; and blissful, innocent Nature, like a serene infant, is too happy to make a noise, except by a few tinkling, lisping birds and trickling rills?

What a place to live, what a place to die and be buried in! There certainly men would live forever, and laugh at death and the grave. There they could have no such thoughts as are associated with the village graveyard—that make a grave out of one of those moist evergreen hummocks!

> Die and be buried who will,
> I mean to live here still;
> My nature grows ever more young
> The primitive pines among.